CHANGE THE RULE

A Guide for Mentoring Young Men of Color

WALTER MENDENHALL IV

Copyright © 2020
Walter Mendenhall IV
CHANGE THE RULE
A Guide for Mentoring Young Men of Color
All rights reserved.

No part of this publication may be reproduced, distributed, or transmitted in any form or by any means, including photocopying, recording, or other electronic or mechanical methods, without the prior written permission of the publisher, except in the case of brief quotations embodied in critical reviews and certain other non-commercial uses permitted by copyright law.

Walter Mendenhall IV

Printed in the United States of America
First Printing 2020
First Edition 2020

10 9 8 7 6 5 4 3 2 1

ACKNOWLEDGEMENTS

First, I would like to thank my Lord and Savior, Jesus Christ, for bestowing me with the opportunity, passion, and drive to deliver this book to the world. I owe a debt of gratitude to my lovely wife, Michelle, for her support and sacrifice for allowing me to pursue my mission in positively transforming the way young people live and lead in their communities. To my mom, for setting the foundation of effectively mentoring and influencing young people. To all my mentors, past and present, especially Coach Joe Galambos, who took an early interest in my development. You truly helped shape me into the man I am today.

My life would not be as fulfilling if every young person I have mentored did not give me the opportunity to influence their lives positively. Thank you. Lastly, I would like to express my appreciation to Patricia Arnold for helping me transform my idea into a published book. I am truly thankful.

This book is dedicated to everyone who wants to be a positive role model and influence the life trajectory of young men of color.

TABLE OF CONTENTS

FOREWORD .... *i*

INTRODUCTION ....*v*

CHAPTER 1 1

Earning the Right To Be Heard

CHAPTER 2 25

The Power of Purpose & Passion

CHAPTER 3 43

The Power of Influence

CHAPTER 4 53

How to Handle Disappointment

CHAPTER 5 67

How to Create Boundaries

CHAPTER 6 79

Unlocking the Shackles

FOREWORD

Few things are as challenging or rewarding as helping a young man of color fulfill his dream and potential. Over the years, America's school-to-prison pipeline has ambushed dreams and flushed them down sewers, particularly in the nation's urban centers. It has thwarted the upward mobility of families, replacing the opportunity for substantial income with criminality for basic survival. When fathers cannot support their families, their hopelessness is more likely to lead to abandonment. It creates a domino effect.

My non-profit organization, and a Ray of Hope on Earth, mentor middle-school boys in four under-served Chicago communities, where most parents do not offer the support and encouragement that are customary in more economically stable neighborhoods. These parents do not attend parent-teacher conferences. They do not volunteer. In fact, they do not even visit their kid's schools unless there's a problem. These parents' disinterest in education typically reflects in their children's low academic performance. Further exacerbating these students' poor outcome is the absence of strong male role models. Nearly 75% of our mentees do not have a father in the home. By default, we have become their father figures, which has intensified our commitment to being credible, consistent models of strong black men.

Knowing this, we often drop by the schools unannounced, just to show that we care. Our unexpected visits are super huge for these guys; it instills a sense of pride. We also try to be there to celebrate their academic victories, no matter how small. Both are immensely important because most young people, particularly boys, are energized by positive affirmation and validation.

Mentoring is the key to success at any age, even for accomplished professionals who want to climb the corporate ladder. For boys of color, it can mean the difference between life and death. There are nuances to mentoring this population, which is why I am so excited that Walter has invested the time and research to create this handbook of insights and best practices to increase the likelihood of positive outcomes for mentors and mentees.

While Walter brings a wealth of experience to this important guide and shares them anecdotally, he also has included tips from other seasoned mentors: Rickie Clark, who has designed, implemented and been involved with numerous mentoring programs for more than three decades, including youth entrepreneurship programs, the Umoja rites of passage program and My Brother's Keeper, an initiative of former U.S. President Barack Obama; Vondale Singleton, assistant principal of a high school on Chicago's South Side and founder of the highly successful Champs mentoring program; and Derrick Fleming, Jr., who stepped onto the mentorship path in college and continues in his role today as the

managing director of the College Access for Chicago Scholars program.

If you are serious about making a difference in the lives of young men of color, but not sure how to get started, how to overcome obstacles or recover from disappointment if your best efforts fail, then this book is for you!

The Rev. Ray McElroy Founder, Ray of Hope on Earth, and 6-year NFL Football Veteran

WALTER MENDENHALL IV

INTRODUCTION

Mentoring young men of color is not for everyone. It's for men who have experienced hurt, overcame challenges and rose above obstacles set before them. This kind of person has something to offer the youth they mentor. These men have real-life experience of how negative situations in the past can evolve into a positive one in the future. They are able to relate to youth, provide strategies for success and walk alongside them through paths they have already taken. A mentor who enjoyed a perfect childhood in a perfect home with perfect parents; who have not been faced with obstacles, experienced no failures, never made a mistake, and does not carry adolescent baggage may not be equipped for this work. I say this because mentoring is not for perfect people and it's not for punks. Mentoring is hard work that requires commitment, empathy and perseverance. This is especially true when considering mentoring youth of color. This is a unique population that deserves special people who truly understand their ordeal and what they go through emotionally, in order to provide what is needed for them to heal and become better.

During the past 12 years as a sports coach, classroom teacher, church leader and founder of a non- profit organization called Male Mogul Initiative Inc. NFP, I have been opportuned to mentor dozens of young men. In my quest to help students of color navigate the obstacles of life, I have encountered and overcome numerous challenges, made countless mistakes and have experienced disappointments when I was unable to push them over the finish line. Early in my mentoring career, I thought I knew everything about mentoring and soon realized that it was a lot harder than I initially thought. I wondered if I had what it took to be a person of influence in the lives of young men. I began to doubt myself until I started to observe mentors around me, even those who had guided me through life. This was when I realized that it wasn't that I didn't possess what these young men needed; it was my process of delivery that needed strengthening. I began to learn lessons and strategies that helped me become more successful at mentoring.

Once I learned a successful approach to mentoring, I wanted to provide those practices with others who shared my passion for doing the same. I developed an effective system that can help other men become positive role models in the areas of education, self-identity, entrepreneurship, family and more. When the right person invests in the life of a youth, I believe they can become successful in all areas of their lives. And when a man experiences success in his life, he can then return that success to his community, city, state, country and ultimately the world.

A man with success and balance can become anything that he wants to despite previous barriers. I am a living example of this very concept. I've encountered a lot of adversity in my life that society would have labeled me a man with no future. These obstacles included a learning disability, single-parent household, below-average economic status, and issues of self-worth. These were situations that could have destroyed me but it did not. Instead, I surpassed other people's expectations of me by graduating college, playing in the NFL, and becoming a successful social entrepreneur.

We are into the new millennium and society has begun to recognize serious concerns with issues that urban young men have to deal with. According to the Pew Research Organization, in 2017, African Americans constituted 2.2 million, or 33%, of the total 6.8 million correctional population. Furthermore, according to The Sentencing Project, African Americans are incarcerated at more than five times the rate of whites in 2017. Not to mention, that nationwide, African American children represent 32% of children who are arrested.

Why is this happening? Well, there are a few reasons to consider.Although barriers for African American families in general have always existed, some are the result of new ones as well. Societal norms, morals and values have dramatically shifted, leaving vagueness in what young people consider between what is right or wrong. Not to mention the public and political discourse on human rights in education, employment and access have coarsened. These new topics often confuse us adults, let alone a youth's perception of what's happening. It can leave them very lost and uncertain, whether a future is even something they should hope to obtain. Which is even more of a reason why they need equipped and consistent mentors in their lives. They need someone with balance, knowledge and experience to guide them into a healthy transition to adulthood.

Many of today's inner-city youth have lived through multiple traumas and disruptive events by the time they begin transitioning to adulthood. They have been victims of abuse and/or neglect, poor preparation or lack of continuity in education, and an array of permanently lost relationships due to premature death. These events are common and unfortunate among youth all over, but more prevalent in urban communities. These harsh experiences can negatively impact the way a youth encounters life. It can lead to problems such as mental illness, substance abuse, inability to peacefully resolve conflict, lack of motivation, loss of self-confidence and no vision. All these are a combination of disastrous life experiences that could have been prevented through the right love, dedication and care that all children deserve.

Unfortunately, some children in the urban community don't have those biological support systems that provide what they need; that's when outside help from mentors can equip and help these young lives with safety security, guidance and most of all, genuine love to become successful no matter the circumstances they find themselves.

While we can see that many young men struggle with these issues, experience has taught me that this is merely a symptom of the root cause: they lack a sense of identity. Complicating matters, researchers say the number of African-American teens who reported that they had attempted suicide is rising, while suicide rates for teenagers of other races and ethnicities have remained steady or decreased. Researchers haven't pinpointed a cause, but I am sure there are several. Whatever the reasons, the need for steady guiding hands for our young people is more urgent than ever. That is why I developed this handbook. I want to multiply the number of mentors and shorten your learning curve to success. My desire is to improve your chances of bringing hope to those who have no hope and create positive outcomes for our young men.

On these pages, you will find best practices, tips, and anecdotes from experienced mentors, including myself. I have provided you with some of my wins and losses so that you can enable their success without disabling yours.

Discussion Questions

1. What do you think it means to be a mentor?
2. Do you have the time and experience to be an effective mentor?
3. How long are you signing up to do this?
4. What are your boundaries?
5. How good are you at listening?

CHAPTER 1

Earning the Right To Be Heard

"No man is a leader until his appointment is approved by the people that he leads."

- John Maxwell

How often do we hear someone complain that teens, especially male teens of color, lack respect? There is an expectation that they should listen to and respect us because we are adults. That expectation emerges from our experience. When we were younger, respecting our elders wasn't optional. Today, many children do not learn to respect elders and others in authority. That dramatically changes the dynamic of our interactions and relationships. Even if we are teachers, administrators, coaches, community leaders or mentors, respect is not guaranteed. If we are of a different race or gender, respect might be intentionally denied as a power play. Despite what we knew of the past, in today's environment, adults and adolescents must earn each other's respect.

Demanding respect from a young person tends to backfire for most adults. Interacting with male youth of color can be challenging because their behavior fluctuates depending on their environment. This can be combated more easily when mentors are consistent and interact with them regularly. Mentors who have continuous engagement with their youth develop respect that can last forever. The impact of their commitment speaks volumes in their life. Ideally, we want to inspire genuine follow-ship, which means that we want them to follow our instructions and stand confident in the guidance we provide for them. We want them to witness us being disciplined, consistent and committed, so they can as well emulate from that. Young people are not just products of their environment, but they are a representation of what they see as well.

Developing trust from a mentee can be difficult because it requires us to engage with young men whose values, life experiences and family situations might be dramatically different from ours, even if we share the same ethnicity. Successful mentors for young men of color don't have to be African American. Young people don't care about what you look like. They care about the benefit and structure you can add to their lives. Any strong mentor can be successful with this demographic of young men as long as they understand that any resistance is not personal but it's from past painful experiences. They have witnessed and experienced many injustices due to systematic racism. They may have been subjected to a few as well. The same is true for many adults in their lives.

As they observe the behaviors and outcomes of their peers and older men in their environments and see so many die or living life unfulfilled, they often anticipate a short and unsuccessful life span. Consequently, they may be unwilling to invest a lot of emotional energy in mentoring relationships, and they are less likely to trust strangers who come into their lives. When teens don't trust you, anyone offering help or asking a simple question such as, "What do you want to be when you grow up?" typically will either not respond at all or nonchalantly answer. Don't be surprised if they maybe even respond with a shrug. It is nothing personal to you; it is just where they are until they experience something greater from any adult. When they have experienced repeated disappointments early, the future is something they can't focus on. They are stuck in their pain, disappointment and exhibit behaviors that are self-destructive due to the affliction that was experienced at the developmental stages of their lives. They simply cannot envision reaching their adulthood because they are presently suffering today, so long term planning is not an option.

It's been my experience that if I present myself authentic, transparent and humble to them, I can begin to earn respect. And if I consistently invest my time, I can begin to find common ground with them. When all of this happens, a genuine relationship building process can begin to flourish. Having them know that I genuinely care about them and proving that I will not leave them will have an impact on our relationship tremendously. They will begin to allow me to guide them to an aspirational future because they know I have their back or interest at heart. Developing trust is huge in working with any young person, but for young men of color it is essential. This group of young men have a cultural, societal and personal predisposition not to trust anyone. So once you have gained it, don't abuse it or it will never occur again.

Derrick Fleming, Jr., a well-known and experienced mentor in the city of Chicago, understands how important it is to gain trust in young people. He has been a mentor for several years and is the Director of College Access for Chicago Scholars, which is a non-profit organization geared towards helping inner city youth receive post-secondary education opportunities. As someone who nearly failed third grade twice, he is keenly aware of the difference mentoring makes in a young person's life. Today, Derrick is the managing director of the non-profit organization College Access for Chicago Scholars. Each year, he works with 30 community-based organizations to help hundreds of students with college admissions. Part of Derrick's work requires mentoring many of these college-bound students and he feels that authenticity is the foundation of effective mentoring relationships. First, he tries to find common ground to begin setting that foundation.

Many may struggle with finding common ground with young people. Finding commonalities can be easier than some may think. Sports and athletics is a good one. No matter if you play, understand or watch sports, any knowledge can be a way in with youth. When I asked Derrick about this he stated, "I was never an athlete. I was never a person that played football or basketball; I liked going to the gym and workout. I just wasn't athletic. I do love sneakers, I love gym shoes and I love fashion. That has been a connecting point for many young folks."

Derrick also loves music, so he listens to what students say they are listening to. But the key, he insists, is authenticity. No matter what the connecting point is, music or fashion, he brings his authentic self to the table every time. Young people are very smart and discerning. They can determine if you are real or telling the truth. So don't try to be something you are not just to connect to them. That can actually push them further away. Derrick even stated that "Young people know when you're being fake and they know that you're not being real." Derrick delivers authenticity and transparency through storytelling. "I share with them experiences I've been through that might be helpful for them. I tell them stories of my peers, colleagues and family members who overcame obstacles. I tell them that there is a possibility that you can be whatever you want to be. You just have to get up and want it." And by consistently communicating this to them and being himself, he has been extremely successful at becoming a very well-known and respected mentor for young men.

Like Derrick, I had to discover my connection points with my mentees. Because I had come from a one-parent home and was an athlete, I assumed that was enough. I thought they simply needed a positive, strong male role model who could tell them how to be successful. My assumption was wrong. When I realized that I didn't have all the answers, I started asking questions to learn more. I simply began to ask them what they needed. I wanted to know how I could better serve and provide them with what they felt was important. I allowed them to open up and express life from their side of the story. That experience was amazing and I learned so much. It humbled me to the point that it changed the way I handled mentorship going forward. It became less about me and more about them.

I learned that our young men need a safe space to openly express themselves, release their anger and simply share their stories with someone who will listen. I learned that by being slow to talk and quick to listen, I could provide them just that. So I began diving into this process more and gained more insight into the lives of young people. This helped me develop stronger and more meaningful relationships with my mentee's over time. The stronger relationships built a foundation for successful mentoring principles in my life. Although there is no tried and specific formula for gaining a youth's relationship, I have developed a formula that has become quite effective for me that I want to share.

Follow these steps, and you should begin to open the doors to a healthy and sincere mentoring connection. It is not complicated at all. It is quite simple. It allows you to be yourself and gives youth the space to do the same:

- Share your story.
- Listen to their story.
- Discern the needs they reveal.
- Be humble.
- Ask questions.
- Encourage feedback.

This is literally how simple it can be to begin. They all are very important to the development of a mentoring relationship. The one I would say can be difficult for some adults is sharing their story. Some people feel that they do not know what they should share with the youth from fear that things could be too harsh or too much for them. Authenticity is what it is. You of course, want to make sure stories are appropriate and clean, but the truth is that this step will begin to break down the barriers of relationship building. Your words, experiences and emotions expressed while revealing your truth will resonate with any listener. I encourage you not to be afraid to be yourself. They need the real you, not the representative to be present.

Everyone has a story, and it might be surprising how a glimpse into our lives can inspire a mentee to open a window into theirs. When I speak to a group of young men or even a group of professionals, I share my story with them no matter what. I share the good, the bad, and the ugly. It is the first step in earning the right to be heard by a large audience but it also is very powerful in launching one-on-one mentoring relationships. In most cases, a young man might not share his story with us until he trusts that we will not judge him, his family or his situation. Whenever I share my story and devote time to listen to a young man's story, a bridge generally appears that leads us to common ground and we can proceed toward common goals. My story starts with what I call the three essential questions to manhood: Who am I? Why do I matter? What is my life's purpose?

WHO AM I?

I began my intense and challenging journey toward discovering what it means to be an African-American man when I was young. I have always been aware of the disparities and obstacles for minorities, but I did not experience it myself until my parents got a divorce. My parents separated when I was five years old and finally divorced when I was nine. Immediately after my father was no longer in our home, I started to feel the direct impact. That impact grew stronger and harsher as I entered my preteen years. This was not only a time that a young man desperately needed their father, but it was also a time when my mother struggled the most.

The comfortable life that I knew began to change. I had to grow up fast and help take care of my family. It was a hard time to live in and very difficult to write about. I am stretching myself by being completely transparent with you so you can do the same with the youth you encounter after this book. So as you read my story, understand that I do not intend on you to feel sorry for me. I desire more that you find something in my words that resonates with you, strengthening your mentoring process. Transparency is the key to developing healthy and trusting relationships with anyone, especially with teens.

My parents were both born into unfortunate yet familiar circumstances for African Americans. My father was one of eleven children that resided in a low-income household in one of Chicago's public housing developments known as the projects. The name of his development was called LeClaire Courts, which was located near Midway Airport on Chicago's southwest side. Growing up in the projects had its pros and cons. On the positive side, it allowed generations of families to live close to each other, allowing for more support during trying times. On the negative side, it created a playground for crime, drugs and gangs as a result of so many poor people residing in the same location. Depending on your family upbringing, influence and mindset, you are left to determine the way you chose to survive there. Unfortunately, my father did not choose the right path. He experienced a lot of tragedies and faced challenges that made his life difficult growing up.

Large families were common among African American families' years ago. My mother had six siblings. Although my mother did not grow up in the projects like my father, her family struggled as well. She grew up with just her mother after her father abandoned them. They lived in poverty and experienced great obstacles on the Southside of Chicago with seven children supported from one income. Things were hard and challenges arose, but she made it through it all. Strength is a commonality from both of my parents.

Despite my parents' troubled beginnings, they both made it through high school and college. They had the determination to push through their environments and wanted to experience life differently than their parents. That tenacity they both had provided a better lifestyle for my brother, sister and I. Our beginnings were very different from that of our parents. When I was a toddler, my father received a technology job in Los Angeles, California. My parents were able to earn high incomes in California. This made life very comfortable for us in our well-furnished two-bedroom apartment. As a child, I remember that apartment seeming so upscale to me. It resembled homes in my favorite TV sitcoms like The Cosby Show and Fresh Prince of Bel Air. I remember feeling great around these times without a care in the world. Life was what it should be in my eyes. I had everything I needed. I felt safe and loved.

Although my parents provided a very comfortable living for our family that was very different from how they grew up, something still was not right. Things were not peaceful and our family started to change. I cannot pinpoint when or why things changed so drastically, but I suspect that my parents' past had something to do with it. They both seemed to have some deep unresolved wounds from their early years that affected their partnership and parenting. Tranquility in our home slowly dissipated. My dad became absent and it caused my parents to argue more. I remember one argument that left an indelible impression. It started in my parents' bedroom. My mom came into the living room where I was watching television. My dad followed and threw a VHS case at her. This surprised me because I had never seen this side of my father before. It was the first and last time I witnessed my father exhibit abusive behavior toward my mother. It terrified me and I will never forget that incident.

My father was almost godlike to me: strong yet gentle, powerful but loving. He has always been a strong disciplinarian, but I deeply loved and respected him. He heavily influenced me. I mimicked his style, his demeanor and his swagger. However, after that argument, I began to develop an unhealthy fear of my father. I was always on edge, never sure what might trigger another violent reaction. This also caused some confusion for me spiritually. Violent experiences can cause trauma for young children. Some things can be healed and some cannot. This one for me affected my outlook on a lot of things, especially my father. We call God "Father." I had learned that the Bible says the father is the priest of his home, a representation of God.

As a consequence, just as I feared my father and harbored resentment, I also developed an unhealthy fear and resentment towards God. I thought that if I made God angry by my actions, He also would lash out in anger. When my natural father left home, I also felt that God would abandon me in the times that I needed him most. I began associating the two as one and the same. So whatever feeling I had for one, I had for the other. Unfortunately, I developed a sense of unworthiness and questioned if God loved me. This was an image of God I subconsciously held onto until my adulthood when I realized to fear the Lord meant to respect or reverence him. God wants us to reverence Him out of love not terror.

Many young men grow up with an unhealthy fear and anger towards God. They simply believe that he does not exist or doesn't care about their life due to relationships or lack thereof with their natural father and the hardship they must face going through life without a man in the home. As mentors, our mentee's may express feelings of hurt, anger, resentment, and fear. But we must be willing to combat all these feelings and emotions with the most powerful emotion of all, which is LOVE.

Shortly after this incident, my father returned to Chicago, leaving us behind in Los Angeles. After his departure, things became financially difficult for my mother, so we eventually came back to Chicago. We moved into my grandmother's home in a low-income area of the city's south side. This was a huge change from what my siblings and I were conditioned to in California. My grandmother was very nice, but not affectionate. I do not remember kissing my grandmother, and only recall hugging her a handful of times. Needless to say, I did not grow up with a lot of affection. This lack of affection became something I tried to deal with in various ways as I entered adulthood.

Even though we were once again in the same city as my father, I can count on one hand the number of times we saw him during our first few months in Chicago. Most of the time, we communicated with him by phone; but those calls were rare. It felt almost as if we were still thousands of miles away from each other. This was difficult to experience and understand as a child.

Now becoming a single parent, my mother had to work harder than she did before to support the family. I remember my mother leaving for work early in the mornings and returning late in the evenings. I missed my mother terribly at these times and it seemed like an eternity before she returned. Her being home made things feel better. My grandmother again was not very engaging and her house was not kid-friendly. We spent most of our days watching PBS shows on an old 12-inch black-and-white TV in what had been my great grandmother's room. Her ashes sat next to the small set. This was a very difficult time for us and a different life to get adjusted to.

My grandmother's neighborhood was not safe, so we did not go outside much. We would stay inside her apartment, which was not comfortable. It was infested with roaches and rats. As a six-year-old at this time, it felt horrifying to experience. I could not be myself there. I could not go outside or even enjoy the beautiful summer activities. For the first time in my life, I was bored and I felt trapped. I often daydreamed about playing with neighborhood kids in Washington Park, across the street from my grandmother's building. Daydreaming was all I could do because it was not a reality for me at all.

We spent about three months there before my mom had enough for us to move out. It was right before the school year was to start. Although this was a great thing to know, it unfortunately was not the last time we had to move. After some time had passed, my parents resolved their differences and reunited. We moved twice more after that, finally settling in Skokie, Illinois. Skokie is a suburb north of Chicago and west of Evanston. It felt like heaven. It was a totally different place from the inner city. Our three-flat apartment building overlooked the canal bordering Evanston. We were able to play in a big backyard. This meant everything to me.

The apartment was spacious, much larger than our home in California. Our family was intact again and I felt secure. I felt like our cohesive unit with love and nurturing was back. The one I had craved since my father left us in California. Life felt as good as the reggae music my parents' blast everyday. My dad was a big reggae fan who played Shabba Ranks's music through our state of the art speakers. Those were great days for us. I never wanted it to end. It was a dream that became a reality. A life full of protection, love and family.

As time progressed, I began to see my parents' relationship deteriorate again. My dad would disappear for days at a time and the arguments became more frequent. I became all too familiar with this pattern. Eventually, they decided it was in their best interest to part ways. They divorced a few years later when I was nine years old. After that, life became a series of broken promises. My dad would call and say he would pick us up. Every time he said those words; it would excite me. I would think about running towards him and greeting him with a big hug whenever he came through the door. That day rarely came. More often than not, the day would grow dark before we realized he was not coming.

Hurt and disappointed, I would cry uncontrollably. I still remember the rejection and sadness on the faces of my mom, brother and even my baby sister those nights. He rarely called to explain why he hadn't honored his promise. I do not even know if he did call, what would he say. What would cause him not to show up for his family. And whenever he did call, he offered no excuses. None. Eventually, we all adjusted. To spare us more disappointment, my mom would not even tell us he was coming until he showed up. By then, it was too late. I was not looking forward to seeing him anymore. On the rare occasions he did show up for the weekend visits, I preferred to have rather stayed at home with my mother.

My story is mine but not uncommon for many African American children. In sharing it, I often find a connection point with mentees who are growing up with an absentee father or with a father who is in the home physically, but not emotionally. The impact on these children is as devastating as it is for children who never see their father. Likewise for children whose father earns an ample salary and refuses to pay child support. They are as deprived as kids whose father is unemployed or underemployed, yet desperately wants to support them financially. One father evokes anger and resentment from his children; the other, expresses understanding and empathy.

Selfishness and cruelty also leave lasting marks on children that mentors may have to help heal. I understand this because on rare occasions when we did see my father; he would always have expensive cars and flash money around. As much as he had, he would never share it with us. Once, he took my brother and I to a Toys R Us store and let us choose a toy we wanted. But when we got to the register, my Dad did not make the purchase. It was such a strange and mean spirited thing to do to kids. Especially your kids. I never quite recuperated from that.

As incidents such as this became commonplace, my young body became consumed with anger and low self-esteem. I felt so unworthy and unloved.. I let a callous grow around my heart so that hurt, disappointment, and even love could not penetrate it. Eventually, it morphed into a distrust of anyone who professed to love me except my mom.

My mother was going through her private hell, doing everything she could to make ends meet. I knew that, so I excused the fact that she had become more emotionally distant and less affectionate after we moved to Chicago. While I knew she loved us deeply, she no longer communicated and rarely hugged or kissed us anymore. She barely had time for us. She was too preoccupied with providing for us and dealing with the divorce. The loss of my father's income required us to move to a more affordable part of town. When we first moved, money was scarce. For a couple of weeks, we did not have much money for food. We often had to share a limited supply of affordable food items such as peanut butter, jelly and hot dogs. We had to do what needed to be done to get through the hard time.

My mother worked two jobs to keep a roof over our heads and food on the table. She arrived home late at night, exhausted. After a few hours' sleep, she was out the door to her other job. By this time, I was nine years old and had become the man of the house. I was responsible for my younger brother, who was seven and my sister, who was three years of age. I cooked food for them, kept them in a clean apartment and put them to bed each night. It felt as if my childhood was over but I was all my mother had. I took my responsibilities very seriously. Maybe too seriously, sometimes.

Once, my brother went to the kitchen to sneak some cookies, I caught him and told him to put them back. He refused and ate them. I grabbed him and proceeded to put the Heimlich maneuver on him until he vomited. Years later, I realized that my violent reaction was the eruption of my deep-seated anger with my father. In reality, I was not upset with my brother; I was mad at my situation. My childhood innocents were gone; my mother was unable to give us the time, attention and affection we deserved because she had to put a roof over our heads. I blamed my father and I had no healthy way to express my anger.

I had no idea then that my mother's lack of affection would have an impact on me in adulthood. I was just a kid afraid of being hurt or abandoned. I was riding an emotional roller coaster, clinging for dear life and no one around me could see or understand. But because I had this experience, I can spot it in other young men. It is almost like an invisible superpower. I believe it has given me credibility so I can help them step out of their pain, feel better, and raise their expectations for themselves. It is ultimately God's way of turning something the enemy meant to destroy me, into something that built me stronger. The stronger I became for myself, the greater I can be for the young men that I serve.

I do not want my mentees to lose any of the time I lost nurturing my resentment. I was unable to establish or maintain healthy relationships with anyone who tried to get too close until I met the wonderful, supportive woman I married. I thought maintaining a safe distance would protect me from pain. I did not realize that unhealthy guarding of my heart would inadvertently hurt me in other ways. My anger and resentment manifested as addictions to illicit behavior. I learned the hard way, and I want my mentees to learn from my mistakes rather than repeat them.

One antidote that I have discovered that has been effective in the inspiration and identity of Black & Brown young men are simple lessons in history. Being a former history teacher, I see young men of color who feel that they have nothing to contribute to society. So I give them the stories of black and brown men who made major contributions to the world: people like Mansa Musa, Ancient Egypt, Timbuktu, Garret Morgan, and Dr. Daniel Hale Williams. I express to them that you come from a rich and powerful legacy and it is up to you to continue the legacy of greatness. That is why I encourage them to ask themselves a critically important question and it is usually the first time they have ever considered it. That question is, "Why do I matter?"

WHY DO I MATTER?

During more than a decade of mentoring, I have asked hundreds of young men of color to answer this question. Few have given me a sufficient answer. When a young man does not know why he matters, he is more susceptible to living life with no intentionality. Those who come from disadvantaged environments and are not intentional with their choices, are more likely to become victims of circumstance.

I have not met a child who was born to be a drug dealer or gang member, but I have met many young drug dealers and gang members who do not know why they matter and were not intentional about their choices. I ask my young men all the time: How much is your life worth? The majority tell me their life is so valuable that they cannot put a price on it. My next question to them is, "If your life is so precious, why do you make decisions that devalue your life?" The majority have no answer. I then share my belief that they are not here by mistake. They are a chosen generation and royalty. Each one is set apart for a great purpose and there is a great plan for their lives. This plan is to prosper them, to give them hope and a future.

"When you live in a community that our kids live in, you know that they get very, very little affirmation of their worth." says former NFL player and master mentor Ray McElroy. "People are really quick to point out where they're missing the mark or where they're messing up or what they need to be doing to be better. Right? They are admonished all the time, but not affirmed enough." He advises us to make sure that we reinforce positive affirmation because our boys need it. Males, in general, need that. I truly believe everyone has a gift to share with the world. Our role as mentors is to help them find and develop their gift. When they develop that talent, it increases the likelihood that they will change their bleak situations for the better, and even make the world a better place.

After focusing my mentees' attention on the life experiences that brought them to this point and helping them realize their self-worth, I generally ask them to ponder one more question. That question is, "What is my purpose?"

WHAT IS MY PURPOSE?

A person's life purpose is often revealed over time. To help my mentee understand that, I generally share how I found mine. I've loved football all my life. Football had become my very essence. Capturing a Rose Bowl ring while at the University of Illinois and being signed by four NFL teams seemed to fulfill my dream. But playing in the NFL was not all that I thought it would be. When I was drafted, I thought all my problems would go away and that I would have peace and fulfillment. That was not the case; It is true that money and fame cannot bring you joy. It can mask your hurt and bring temporary relief to your suffering. It can also give you access to many vices that promise to make you happy but in the end, it can destroy your life and everything that you worked for.

Although I loved playing professional football, my time in the NFL was involuntarily done like most men in the athletic profession. My life-long obsession with becoming an NFL star soon faded away and I was depressed because I had no idea who I was outside of sports. Sports was where I got my positive affirmation and self-worth. When I was no longer an athlete, I dealt with depression until I began discovering a higher calling and purpose for my life. Even though I still loved the game, I began to see a bigger picture. That bigger picture was educating youth.

My first jump into this new life was gaining a position as a paraprofessional educator and coach at a high school in the Chicago area and it was there that I realized that I had a gift of positively influencing young men. I worked during the day and was a graduate student at National Louis University by night. It required a lot of late nights and early morning homework sessions. Even though I had been diagnosed with a learning disability, the same positive attitude and mental discipline that served me so well in football paid off again in school. Upon receiving my Master's Degree in Education and Social Sciences, I began teaching in the inner city of Chicago. This was a great experience that led me to my true calling. This was what I was born to do. This was my purpose.

In all my formative years, I never saw myself as a teacher. But there I was, teaching the next generation. Standing in front of a classroom, I not only realized my gift, but I was also able to see how much I had to give. I had a new passion: to impact lives through education and mentoring. The transition from football to education showed me how life works. I realized that nothing is permanent. As life proceeds, things change and you have to adjust to it the best way you can. Life is 10% of what happens to you and 90% on how you respond to it.

I learned that whatever struggle I am going through is only temporary and that I will get through it. This realization changed my life. It was through serving others that I began to fill a void I felt for most of my life. It gave me peace, happiness, and satisfaction. However, in my new teaching role, I still found myself searching for a more impactful way to work with young people. Even though the school where I taught had a great mission and a spiritual component that made a difference in the lives of the kids, I was missing something. I wanted to do more outside the classroom. I wanted to work with the youth in a different way and where they needed it more. Ironically, it was a teenager who pointed me in the right direction.

One day while teaching my sophomore world history class, a student asked, "Mr. Mendenhall, have you ever thought about motivational speaking, like on the videos you show us?" It threw me off for a second. I remember asking him, "Do you really think people would want to hear me speak?" And with all the assurance in his voice, he stated to me, "I would listen to you!" And that was enough for me. What an eye-opener. That year, I paid closer attention to the impact I was having on my students, particularly those I was mentoring. I became keenly aware that some of them were experiencing exponential growth, both academically and behaviorally.

I discovered that keeping these young men engaged and motivated, letting them know how success and education work together, and using my life lessons as examples made a tremendous difference. That inspired me to make a significant difference in the lives of a greater number of young men of color. One way I am doing that is through speaking engagements nationwide. I travel anywhere that youth call me to.

Anywhere that I can make a difference in a young person's life. I allow my voice to be the driving force of hope, confidence and reassurance that life can be better. The other is by helping others who mentor to become successful by creating this handbook. I know I cannot be everywhere all the time. So I plan to train and build up as many mentors as I can to do what needs to be done. Mentors in training need a master mentor who can lead and guide them to become powerful, effective mentors and teachers. I am passionate about this craft and want to see people who have the heart to do the job well succeed truly. I am that person who has dedicated his life to the empowerment of mentors and mentees to be the best version of themselves.

Discussion Questions

1. How do you earn the right to be heard? (six steps to healthy mentoring)

2. What are the three essential questions to manhood? And why are they important to the development of a young man?

3. How can we assist young men in discovering the three essential questions of manhood?

WALTER MENDENHALL IV

CHAPTER 2

THE POWER OF PURPOSE & PASSION

The greatest tragedy in life is not death, but life without reason.
~Dr. Myles Munroe

I cannot emphasize enough the importance of discovering and connecting with our purpose. During my teaching career, I realized that students who were disrupting my class or having difficulty reading did not have a reading or behavioral problem; they had a purpose problem. They had no positive direction. When youth do not understand their purpose, they can not understand why certain things need to be done. This generation is a "Show Me" generation. They want to know why and have it shown before they act. This is because of past letdowns and disappointments. They have developed natural unbelief of everything. I believe it is my place

as an educator and mentor, to help them believe. If they do not believe in anything else, they have to believe in themselves.

In one of my favorite books, Unleash Your Purpose, Dr. Myles Munroe wrote, "The deepest craving of the human spirit is to find a sense of significance and relevance. The search for relevance in life is the ultimate pursuit of humankind." For Munroe, this pursuit for purpose is our only source of fulfillment. Without purpose, he felt, life has no meaning. It is the master of motivation and the mother of commitment, the source of enthusiasm and the womb of perseverance. Purpose gives birth to hope and instills the passion to act. That passion is what every young person needs to achieve their goals. It will pull them through hard times and keep them striving in good times. It will be what helps them to breakthrough to obtain their goals and get what they want out of life instead of being complacent with what they currently have.

As humans, our limitations live mostly in our minds. As children, our dreams and possibilities are limitless. As we get older, we limit our possibilities and dreams based on what our environment, family, media, friends, and those in authority tell us. There is a deep need in communities of color to introduce and expose our young people to the countless opportunities and career paths available. Until then, it is difficult for mentors to inspire a generation of young people to follow in the footsteps of successful individuals and realize their true potential.

As a teacher, it was disheartening to witness the disparities between what the educational system and the media present to young people. There was a continuous celebration of accomplishments of white men without similar mentions of those made by black and brown people. The most acclaim or any recognition given to minorities was in entertainment and sports. Although these amazingly talented people should be celebrated for their gifts, African Americans are more than just entertainers. African Americans simultaneously have contributed greatly in the areas of politics, social justice, education, healthcare, law and many areas of importance. Those faces who achieved greatness in these areas are not given the same opportunities as their mainstream counterparts.

The subliminal message transmitted to students of color is not only that white men are responsible for every significant advancement mankind has made, but persons of color are not as smart or capable. Young people then set their educational achievement, income, and career

expectations to match society's low expectations. This creates quite a hurdle for mentors to help them catapult. Even conscientious, well-meaning teachers who hold no racial biases sometimes only see life through the lens of a white male world view unless they studied African- American or Latinx-American history, so it's unlikely they will detect the true source of their students' defeatism.

I believe hopelessness is a fate worse than death for young men of color. It lasts throughout their lifetimes and dooms them to sub-par quality of life. Reversing this pervasive hopelessness became my top priority. While I enjoyed teaching and found it a noble profession, I knew I had to do something different and more far-reaching. I felt called to inspire a generation to realize their potential and expand their vision to see what is possible in their lives. That calling led me to reflect on another Munroe truism: "Until purpose is discovered, existence has no meaning."

The lives and living conditions of one community can spill over and impact an entire city. Consequently, it's in everyone's best interest to invest in the viability, safety and quality of life in disadvantaged communities because they are not isolated from our own. The self-worth of a young person in a disadvantaged neighborhood influences their valuation of others' lives. In fact, the value of our existence diminishes when a young person has no destiny or purpose in his viewfinder.

I say this authoritatively because I have mentored dozens of young men who suffer from an acute case of cynicism and pessimism. They barely live because each day they anticipate death. Their cynicism stems from feeling nothingness and witnessing hopelessness. I see my role as helping them see themselves and live differently. If they see more possibilities, their self- image improves. I have worked with young men whose outlook dramatically shifted after being inspired to search for and fulfill their unique purpose.

Our purpose as mentors is to help them accomplish their successes in life by sharing our stories. Our stories and in-depth. Search for purpose can inspire them to do the same in their lives. As I stated before, children are more than the environment they grow up in but also a representation of what they see. Witnessing other men who look like them succeed and understanding the pathway it took them to reach that success, can do wonders for a young person's outlook on life. That is our job as mentors and teachers. Our role is to lead, model and teach by experience.

Our next step is to say nothing. Just listen. We often assume we know the needs of male teens because we come from similar backgrounds or even the same gene pool. Understand that we will not fully know their need or what they perceive to be their needs until they tell us, and we listen with an open heart. Like all of us, young people have an innate need to be heard. When adults listen, we not only demonstrate that our mentees' concerns matter to us;

we genuinely show respect for them. By listening, the subsequent conversations become clearer and more straightforward. If we have been consistently transparent, mentees will be able to mirror our transparency, and each of us will take another step towards fulfilling our life purpose.

How do we take that step with a young man seeking his purpose in life? I have developed a formula that has been effective for me. It combines the role of passion in one's success with using our gifts and talents wisely to discover our unique purpose. Although I do not have all the answers, I have asked enough questions in my career to set the foundation for what you will need. I did everything I am trying to teach you to do and it has worked. I am successful in mentoring. My success is not for me to brag. It is for the lives of every young man that I have encountered who is now an adult. Adult's that are full of hope and have a desire to achieve their goals no matter what they were up against growing up. A grown man who loves himself, his life and those he allowed in his life. A man who knows his purpose and is living in it. This is my greatest life work that I want you to experience as well.

PASSION'S ROLE IN SUCCESS

Passion is pivotal to purpose. It gives us fuel to stay the course. It inspires us to push our boundaries, sometimes beyond what we might have considered possible. We will tackle the most difficult tasks when we love what we are doing. That's why I always ask new mentees, "What are you passionate about? What would you do free of charge?" When I was a teenager, my only passion was sports. That passion drove me to aim for a big goal: playing professionally. I knew I could not achieve that goal unless I worked hard in other areas, academics in particular. Sports motivated me to excel academically because good grades could lead to a college athletic scholarship.

My passion also steered me away from major distractions and bad life choices. When I experienced momentary distractions or made poor choices, my purpose refocused me on what was really important. Challenges did come that made me second guess or wonder if I was doing the right thing. At times, I did not know what step I was going to take. All I knew was what I considered to be my passion and it brought me joy, gave me everything I needed in life. So instead of allowing my fears of failure or self-doubt drive me insane, I took a step anyway. Moving forward, no matter what I was experiencing always led me in the right direction. The worst thing you can do is stand still. Standing still is too close to going backwards. No one achieves greatness by going backwards.

USING GIFTS AND TALENTS WISELY

As mentors, I feel it is our role to help them discover and appreciate their gifts, develop and fine-tune them, and ultimately profit from them. When speaking about gifts and talents with a group of teens individually, I often share the biblical parable of the talents. Of course, teens are rarely open to a "Bible conversation," so I simply relate a story about a king who gave three servants a gift of money. I explain that every country has its name for its currency. In that kingdom, they called their gold coins "talents." The king gave one servant five talents; the next servant was given two talents, and the last servant was given one talent. He sent them away with instructions to put their money to good use.

A long time later, the king called the three servants to report what they had done with their gifts. The first servant said, "Your majesty, I have all the money you gave me and more: I put my five talents to good use and now I have ten." The king nodded, "Excellent, faithful and trustworthy servant. You may keep all of it." The second servant said, "I also increased the money you gave me, Sir. I invested my two talents and now I have four. The king again nodded, "Good! You invested it wisely!" He then turned to the last servant. "What have you done with the talent I gave you?" The third servant replied, "Sir, I know you are a hard and strict man, and I did not want to lose the talent you gave me. I kept it in a safe place so I could return it to you whenever you asked." The king was furious. "How lazy! I blessed you with a chance to become prosperous, and you did nothing with it? I am disappointed in you!" To the guards standing by, he ordered, "Banish this man from my sight and give his talent to the one who has ten!" After telling this story, I ask my mentee why the king sent the third servant away. The answer is very clear to them: that servant wasted his talent.

I then ask, "Do you know people who have wasted their talent?" They always do and they do not want to be that person. I then ask them a more difficult question. "Why do you think the king gave the talent to the servant who returned with ten, and not to the one who had five?" That question typically stumps them. I then explain that people want to help those who are less fortunate but they also want to see a return on their investment. In other words, when someone helps you, they want to see you win. The more promise and results that a young person demonstrates, the more people will want to invest in them. At this point, I can see the light in their eyes. They have a spark of inspiration to make the most of the gifts they have been given—just as I did when I was their age.

I clearly remember the day in ninth grade when a coach told me I was good enough to land a football scholarship to college. It was the day everything changed. At 14 years old, I did not see myself as a college football player, or in college! I knew I loved playing the game. I also excelled on the track team. Basketball was my passion but my future was in football. Football has always been my younger brother, Rashard's, gift. He was the star athlete in that sport. His skills made playing football with him great. We were a powerful backfield combination for our high school.

When that coach told me I was worthy of a football scholarship. He ignited a dream and passion and gave me hope and insight on what I could possibly do; I began to see the game differently. I became very deliberate in developing my talent. I worked out every day before school. I studied the game by watching films. I maximized every opportunity, on and off the field, to ensure that I was eligible to play in every game. I performed my best during each game and maintained good standing academically. I tried my best to stay out of trouble. I made sure my body was prepared mentally and physically to perform at its peak. Eventually, it paid off!

I received a scholarship to the University of Illinois. This was so exciting for me. I felt as if I had accomplished something I never thought I could. Now that I had reached that goal, I had to make another. I did not want to be just another athlete. I wanted to be the best. And I strived for that everyday at the University of Illinois on and off the field. Between 2005 and 2007, I played thirty-one games as a running back, linebacker and performed on special teams. I was named the offensive star of our spring 2006 game. My brother Rashard was also topping Illinois' rushing-yard records. The next year, together we won the Big Ten Conference and the Rose Bowl. This was a huge accomplishment for me. I felt so happy because I set my mind to something, and I successfully achieved it all.

I began to wonder, where would this football talent take me? With the same determination, I set my sights on playing professionally. I had it in my heart that the NFL was where I wanted to be. I knew I had the talent to achieve my goal; all I needed was the opportunity to showcase my ability. It was my plan to showcase that ability in my senior year at the University of Illinois, but when I picked up my Rose Bowl ring, the head coach told me I was not in the Fighting Illini's future plans. This meant that they did not want me to play my last eligible college season. I was stunned and devastated. I was completing my degree that year and I still had a year of eligibility left. I could not understand why this was happening to me but I knew my dream was still my dream. I was going to the NFL.

CHANGE THE RULE

After I graduated undergraduate school, I entered graduate school at Illinois State. I began playing football again and I performed extremely well. Despite only starting the last four games of the season, I achieved a lot there. I rushed for more than 800 yards that year and gained 11 touchdowns. After the season, I showcased enough potential to enter the NFL draft. I

felt validated that the belief in my abilities were correct. I used the rejection and setbacks at the University of Illinois as a motivation to catapult me to my goal of being in the NFL.

When my college career ended, surprisingly, I was on the NFL's radar. They were starting to take notice in my craft but I wasn't drafted. This was when Sports Illustrated professed me as one of its "small school draft sleepers." This meant that they followed my career and saw it worthy enough to be in the professional league despite my lack of statistics. That mention alone began to ring bells for others. Being featured in one of the world's most respected athletic publications was one of the best highlights in my football career. Eventually, I signed to play with the Philadelphia Eagles as an undrafted free agent.

Living the dream and reaching my goal of playing in the NFL was achieved. It felt great to accomplish this goal, but it did not last long for me in Philadelphia. A few months into my time there, they waived me. Being waived in the NFL means removing a player from a team and releasing him from his contract. After I was waived, The Indianapolis Colts signed me. Within a month, they waived and re-signed me and waived me again. But at least I got to play three pre-season games while clinging to that roller coaster.

The professional football rollercoaster was not over yet for me. The following year, the Buffalo Bills signed me, and later, the Cincinnati Bengals. Both waived me after about a month. Eventually this ride became too much and it was showing me something I could not ignore. It was clear that although I had talent and passion for the game, playing professional football was not my destiny or my purpose. It was not even the means through which I would discover my purpose. At that time, I had no idea what the future without football held for me. All I knew was that I had a degree without a football career. The worst part for any professional athlete or any person is working your whole life for something and in an instant, it is gone.

At 24 years of age, that was a lot to deal with; I no longer had structure and direction in my life. I did not know what to do or where to go. I struggled to find self-worth outside my football player identity. I had no purpose; I was lost. One day I received a surprise call from my former high school coach, Mr. Egofske. We had not spoken in years. He asked if I would consider a football coaching role at the high school that was our former rival. I was still obsessed with making it in the NFL. I never considered coaching, but was this the right move for me? I told him I would think over it. I knew I had to do something. Maybe coaching would keep me connected to the game until the next NFL team called. It was worth looking into.

WHEN PASSION MEETS PURPOSE

Days later, I returned Coach Egofske's call. My answer was yes; I would like to coach with him. I had no idea what a life-altering decision I had made. It quickly dissolved the doubt, insecurity and confusion around my disappointing efforts to have a career as a professional football player. More than that, it set me on a more fulfilling and more purposeful path as a coach and mentor. My first day with the team, I discovered that the young men were very different from high school teens a mere five years earlier. There was no light in their eyes. They had no passion for success, and some were very difficult to communicate with. Their values were remarkably different than when I was a teen. So many were lost, and no one was helping them find their way.

As the school year progressed, so did I. I began to feel a natural gift emerge from within. It felt powerful, exciting and endearing. This gift gave me confidence in my approach with the youth. I was actually making headway with those hard to reach kids. We got along well and they were allowing me to influence them in positive ways. I can only conclude that even though we did not share the same values, I still saw in them a younger version of myself. Some of them came from the same or worse background; they faced the same emotional battles I had at their age. I felt perfectly positioned to help them.

Coaching was a door that slowly opened to a place of joy and belonging. Working with these kids returned me to the foundation I had built so many years ago through all my hard work and perseverance. If I am giving the impression that it was easy, it was not. It was a frustrating first season before I formed great relationships with my players. It was difficult for these kids to put their faith in me. They had learned during early childhood not to trust anyone and to be as tough as possible. Every moment I spent with these kids was amazingly liberating. This liberation relieved me of the burden I carried wanting to be in the NFL. My shoulders were lighter. I felt free. I was no longer preoccupied with what the future might hold for me because I was so invested in their futures. Coincidentally, investing in their futures became my future.

One year earlier, I had been completely consumed with establishing a permanent position in the NFL. I was bouncing from team to team, not knowing where I would end up. To my surprise, I had no idea that I had ended up where I was supposed to be. Although I had a good time playing professional football for a limited time, it was not what I needed to do. I was using my talents now coaching and mentoring vulnerable kids. That role eventually led to a full-time position as a paraprofessional in the school's special education department. This was somewhere I never envisioned that I would be. Although I never considered this profession, it was exactly where I wanted.

In my new role, I observed firsthand what experts have identified as a systemic problem plaguing school systems across America. Most of the young people in my special education classes were students of color, even though Black and Latinx students comprised only 22% of the school's population. This really alarmed me because so many of these students clearly were as intelligent as their white classmates. They were simply unmotivated and angry. I wondered: Who labeled these kids as special education students? Why were they not given access to the same level of educational challenges I'd been given, less than a decade earlier? Why were the behavioral and academic expectations for these kids so low?

The answers to some of those questions unfolded during a troubling incident in a school hallway. One of my athletes was poised to assault a teacher, an older woman before I intervened. I reported the incident, but nothing was done. In fact, the young man was on the court the following Friday. I was stunned. That is when I realized that the school was rewarding misbehavior. Sometimes it appeared that they specifically ignored discipline for the exchange of obtaining athletic celebrity. The administration was more invested in winning games than producing well-educated young men of color who would be assets to society. These students had no incentive to behave maturely, resolve conflict peacefully or succeed academically. They were being set up for failure in the real world where the school could not protect them. It was devastating to witness.

I became preoccupied with the exponential number of victims this pattern of miseducation was creating. How many innocent lives, inside and outside the black and brown communities, are harmed by the school system? Our schools are supposed to be educating and developing young people for the world ahead. They should be guiding them into being productive citizens who are ready for college, careers or society. Instead, they were holding them back from healthy development into experiencing a life of success. They were teaching them how to ignore responsibility, disrespect authority and avoid accountability for their actions.

After witnessing that incident, I was infused with a new passion to address the issue. I wanted to change the negative systematic outcomes for male students of color and their potential by leveraging my athletic ability, interpersonal gifts and leadership abilities. Out of my frustration, I discovered my purpose. It was not to be content with being a part of a system that I felt was destructive. One that is using rather than uplifting students of color. So I decided to walk away from the highest paying school district in the state to fulfill my purpose. To me, money and notoriety was worth less than creating a positive structure for young people that looked like me. I wanted to do more and make a real difference. My journey for more began.

Since making that decision, I have mentored hundreds of young people through various youth empowered organizations.. I even started my own organization called the Male Mogul Initiative, which introduces young men to entrepreneurship and leadership development. Through my organization, I am able to teach young men of color how to develop, own and operate their businesses. I also travel speaking to groups of young men across the nation. I continued to coach youth in sports because there are a lot of foundational principles that athletics provides. Reaching the older youth as much as I could, I began to also teach in college classrooms. Out of everything that I have done and continue to do to restructure the perception of the future for males of color, I believe education is the most important. Teaching appears to be my foundation on which I receive the most success. I can reach more from teaching what I know and have experienced, which is why I am currently pursuing a doctorate in organizational leadership.

HELPING TEENS SEARCH FOR PURPOSE

The route to my purpose was circuitous; perhaps yours was more of a straight line. Regardless if it was different, our shared purpose is to uplift young men of color. We desire to help those who live in vulnerable households and communities to become great. Our greatest challenge is to inspire them not only to search for their purpose but to fulfill it. Mentees often find their purpose tucked inside their talents. They can fulfill it through activities they are most passionate about, or by solving a societal, consumer or business problem, they consider important.

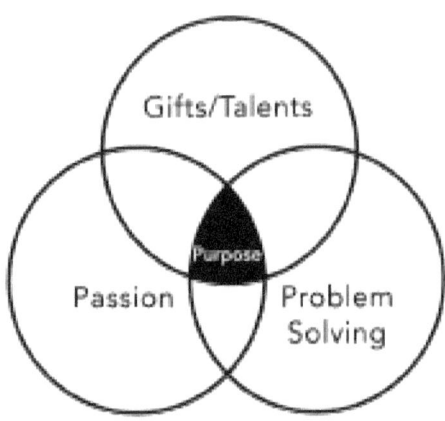

As mentors, our role is to encourage them to consciously conduct a meaningful search. They might hesitate or resist because, if they are like my students and mentees, they already have endured a lot of hurt and disappointment in their young lives. They have lost close friends and family members, so they doubt if life has any good thing to offer them.

I always acknowledge and respect my cynical mentees' hurtful experiences. But I also tell them that my trials and tribulations have built muscle. Adversity has been a blessing to me and millions of others because it has made us stronger.

I then suggest that when they are strong enough, they will have the power to transform their pain into healing for themselves and others. Adversity, failure and disappointment can be a pathway for people to discover the purpose of their lives and it can help them see the value of their lives and that of every human being. I know this seems like a "which came first: the chicken or egg" situation. Admittedly, it is cyclical. But I have witnessed the reaction of hardened young men when they realize how their perception of themselves influences others' perceptions of them. It only takes a simple question, "If you don't believe your life has a purpose or that your life matters, how do you expect others to believe it does?"

Discussion Questions

1. Why is purpose and the understanding of purpose so powerful for a young man?
2. Why is it important to not but your self-worth or identity in temporary exploits?
3. How can your passion lead you to your purpose?
4. How can you assist your mentee in the pursuit of Purpose?

CHAPTER 3

THE POWER OF INFLUENCE

"Leadership is influence. Nothing more, nothing less."
John Maxwell

Each of us is susceptible to multiple influences through our relationships, our conversations, advertising, books or social media, news stories, movies we watch or scenes we witness in real life. The closer we are to others, physically or virtually, the greater their influence over us, and vice versa. We can easily recall how our high school friends, family members, teachers and coaches influenced us. Those experiences were either positively or negatively. No matter what they were, they had a direct impact on us. "I believe more things are caught than taught," mentor, minister and former NFL player Ray McElroy reflects. "It is amazing how boys see stuff that we do not even realize they are looking at. You never know who is watching you."

As mentors, our influence can change the course of someone's future. Our mentees observe what we do and how we do it. Their parents, coaches, teachers, administrators, siblings and friends are also keeping a watchful eye. Perhaps that is why the New Testament of the bible in Timothy 4:12, calls on us to be positive influences "in speech, in conduct, in love, in faith and in purity." This means that it is our responsibility to be a positive force in each other's lives. This is even truer for adults to do for children. It is our responsibility as adults to guide the next generation in the right way of life. In order to do that, we must first know what that is and exemplify it in everything that we do. Our influence should be positive and beneficial to everyone watching us.

BECOMING A GOOD INFLUENCE

We may aspire to resist being swayed by others' emotions or actions. The reason most of us are unable to resist this influence may lie in a principle Buddhists call the oneness of life and its environment. In other words, we are constantly and unconsciously influencing our environment, and our environment is constantly influencing us. When explaining the pervasive nature of influence and impressing upon young people the importance of choosing their peer groups wisely. Some have conflated this principle with an adage popularized by motivational speaker Jim Rohn: We are the average of the five people with whom we spend the most time.

This can be more confusing than constructive. After all, who constitutes "the average" when three friends are wealthy and two are struggling financially—or when four friends are outstanding athletes and one barely made the team? Wealthy friends can influence or inspire the struggling ones to set their sights higher and work harder. Gifted athletes can do the same for their friend who lacks their natural talent. But no one is truly "the average" of their closest friends.

I prefer offering young men the challenge posed by writer Moosa Rohat: "Show me your friends, I'll show you your future." It is easier for them to visualize how their close friends are influencing their success. I remember one of my mentors challenging me to access the people I called friends. Two weeks before my 8th-grade graduation. My basketball coach and dean of students called me into his office. He told me, "Walter, you have all the potential in the world but your friends are going to be your downfall." At the time, I tried to ignore his warning, but in the summer of 8th-grade year, my friends decided to become gang affiliated and I struggled with the choice of associating myself with such a dangerous group.

That August, those same friends decided to join the football team at our high school. After the second day of practice, they wanted me to quit and go with them to smoke weed and also talk to girls. At the age of 14, I made the most important decision that I ever made in my life. I stayed at the football practice and they left. Out of the eight people at my 8th-grade lunch table, only two of us stayed in high school all four years and graduated and I was the only one that went to college. My life trajectory would be a lot different if I left football practice with my friends.

Rohat's influence challenge applies to anyone, including mentors. We, too, should choose our associates wisely by surrounding ourselves with reputable and respectful individuals who have strong personal and professional relationships. Those that exhibit positive attitudes, are generous with their time, uplift others and contribute to their communities. This would make us all successful and continuously striving to be the best version of ourselves daily.

In 1970, the term "servant-leader" entered our vernacular after educator and leadership consultant Robert K. Greenleaf published an essay entitled, "The Servant as Leader." In that essay,

Greenleaf said: "The servant-leader is the servant first. It begins with the natural feeling that one wants to serve, to serve first. Then conscious choice brings one to aspire to lead. That person is sharply different from someone who is a leader first. This is perhaps because of the need to assuage an unusual power drive or to acquire material possessions." This statement spoke to me deeply and changed the way I looked at leadership. What stands out for me in Greenleaf's definition of a servant-leader is the natural feeling to prioritize service to others. In other words, leading from the heart.

The most effective mentors have a servant's heart. They are patient, kind, slow to anger and keep no records of wrongs, matching Paul the Apostle's definition of love. They also collaborate with people they may not like to resolve conflict. Dr. Martin Luther King Jr, Nelson Mandela and Mahatma Gandhi are classic examples. These amazingly great leaders did not hate those that opposed them. Instead, they loved everyone and showed them how to do the same. They lived on the principles that everyone deserves happiness, justice and love. No one was treated better or differently than the other. Everyone was respected, considered and recognized for greatness. They served those less fortunate than them and did it with complete honor and humbleness because they were not prideful and had pure intentions.

It has been my experience that when we have a servant's heart, young people feel it. They muster the strength to tear down the emotional and psychological walls they have constructed to protect themselves. They become less fearful of being vulnerable. They begin to trust. They begin to listen. They allow their mentors to serve them and truly make a difference in their lives. I not only highly recommend servant leadership for all mentors but I urge mentors to surround themselves with other servant leaders. They will influence you to be the best kind of leader; likewise, you will influence them. The benefits will grow exponentially with each life you touch.

I do not know about you, but I do not believe I am on Earth by accident. I honestly believe God placed me here with a purpose. I am here for reasons greater than I can imagine and reasons that will transcend my time on this earth. I also believe that I will fulfill my God given purpose through my interactions and relationships with God's human family. Your beliefs may be different, and that's perfectly fine. Each of us decides what to believe. However, we all need to be consciously aware of our beliefs because they heavily influence the way we treat others.

When I was a high performing college athlete, no one could have convinced me that a Hall of Fame professional football career was not my destiny. But it was not. I worked relentlessly to achieve that dream and I did not receive it. I made it to the front door but could not get in. This was hard to realize but once I did, my life continued to move in a great direction. Once I discovered that my destiny was to make a positive difference in young men's lives, I detected a noticeable shift in my life. I had renewed passion: to fulfill my God given purpose. Instead of focusing on my dreams, I focused my energy on supporting others to realize their dreams. Without realizing it, I was gradually becoming a servant leader.

Even though servant leadership might emerge naturally, it also requires a concerted effort to act responsibly. A leader must take responsibility for any way they have contributed to the problems around us. Case in point: While the senseless killings of young men and women of color are alarming and disheartening, I do not feel personally responsible for their deaths. However, every death reminds me that I must do whatever I can to help minimize or alleviate the conditions that trigger violence. I willingly take responsibility for this and work to encourage young men of color to make choices that give them an opportunity. Your words have great power! Use them to build up the youth.

In fact, I believe our words can hold the power of life and death for a young person. So many of our young men lack encouragement from adults who are successful in their trades or professions. It is meaningful when we tell them, "You are not here by accident. You are here to accomplish something great!" If we say this often enough with sincerity and conviction, our mentees will begin to believe it. They will believe it because they see us investing our most precious asset in them, and also our time. This demonstrates that they are worthy of our time and that we care about their development. We build their trust every time we show up and are responsive to their outreach.

Many teens, particularly those from under-resourced communities, are skeptical of adults who are not familiar to them. Whether we enter their lives as a new teacher, coach or mentor, we must be mindful that they are watching you closely. Vondale Singleton, Founder of Champs Mentoring, believes that this observance is done early on in life with children. He stated the following, "I think a lot of people lose credibility when they do not follow through with what they said. It started with a father who reneged on his promise to take them to an amusement park, buy new shoes or ice cream. A kid who was full of hope at four and five turns into a monster by fourteen, fifteen and sixteen.

By the time we meet him, he has walls up because he had been hurt by his first superhero. Now, he is taking it out on kids at school. He is angry with mom, and people do not know why." We have a chance to break the cycle by demonstrating that men can have integrity. We can do that by always telling the truth and always honoring our word. "We're trying to really teach these boys what it looks like to be masculine," says McElroy "Masculinity is not the ability to knock somebody out because they got on your nerves. Sometimes, it is meekness and it is strength under control."

Being honorable and having strong moral principles are the best ways for mentors to positively influence young men. We must have character, practice what we preach, and consistently engage them authentically. We must be real and keep it real, especially with young men of color. If we approach them with humility by meeting them where they are and accepting them as they are, we will be in a position to inspire them to reach for something greater.

In summary, every mentor's ability to be a positive influence requires a willingness to be a servant leader, as well as a role model. Character, integrity, humility, credibility, trustworthiness, and authenticity matter. These personal qualities are deeply impactful in the lives of young people. It is as important for mentors to choose peers who reflect these characteristics and who support the work we are doing as it is for our mentees to choose their associates wisely. Remember, all of our environments influence us and they influence the outcomes of mentoring relationships. Everything and everyone that consumes much of our time, physical and emotional energy is important to healthy relationships with youth. Time and energy spent with a mentee is an investment. We want to earn a return on that investment, and we want it to pay off greatly for the young men we serve. We ultimately want our lives to be a mirror for what theirs should look like. We are the man they want and will be when we do our job to the best of our ability

NAVIGATING GENDER IDENTITY ISSUES

At some point, all mentors will face a critical test. They must know how to respond when mentees ask for help addressing their gender identity. It is a reality with youth in society right now and it is important how all adults handle it. I received the best insight on this from Derrick Flemming, a seasoned mentor that I know. When students disclosed to him that they are interested in others of the same gender, his first response is to ascertain how best to support them. He does that by asking about their emotional and psychological state. He does not focus on what was said but more of what was not. His first desire is to understand how they are feeling about this new self-discovery. How they feel inside about themselves is what ultimately matters most regardless of the situation.

It is inevitable that a mentor will have to deal with identity issues in this current generation. This is a time when society is more accepting of differences in sexual orientation of all ages. This means that mentors must educate themselves about the concept and how to handle it when it comes up. They can do so through Diversity, Equity and Inclusion (DEI) training, seminars or workshops addressing young people's challenges in lifestyle changes. "When it comes to the LGBT community, we must understand the pronouns and everything involved with that," he says. "When you are encountering something new, you always want to make sure you are educated if you are going to be a successful and effective leader."

Discussion Questions

1. What is influence and why is it important in mentorship?
2. How do you become a positive influencer?
3. What is servant leadership in your own words?
4. What does servant leadership look like to you?
5. What are the steps to effectively navigating a mentee that is struggling with gender issues?

CHAPTER 4

How to Handle Disappointment

"Every young man is born to win in every situation in life. Two parent home, one-parent home; you live a life with no excuses."
Vondell Singleton, Champs Mentoring Program

Mentoring relationships are not different from personal ones when disappointment is concerned. In our personal relationships, things are not always perfect. We invest time and energy in people with the expectation that our commitment will see positive rewards. We expect everyone to understand our perspective on various issues, and for them to adhere to our suggestions. But in reality, it rarely goes that way and we have to readjust or find another way to deliver our message effectively. This cycle often leaves us disappointed and frustrated. Personal relationships typically do not live in a disappointment-free zone.

Mentoring relationships are no exception. In fact, they can be more susceptible to disappointments due to the amount of time mentors invest, the experienced-based advice we share with our mentees, and the exposure to new possibilities and opportunities we provide our mentees. In fact, mentors may experience more disappointments because no matter how much you teach someone something, the decision to do better is still theirs. When mentees make decisions that we do not agree with, mentors may feel that the amount of time you invested, the wisdom you have shared and the exposure you have provided them, were all in vain.

Longtime mentor Derrick Fleming, Jr. recalled a situation he encountered that is a perfect example of how a mentor can experience disappointment in their mentees' decision making. As the managing director of a not-for-profit organization that facilitates college access for students from under-served communities, Fleming has mentored several young men. In this situation, there were two young men that he was mentoring for nearly four years. They were both great leaders in their school and very well aware of their mentor's expectations from them. One day, he received a shocking call from the school, stating that both boys were involved in a physical altercation.

"It did not make any sense," Fleming recalled. He remembers rushing to the school desperate to find out what happened. "I had to first check myself because I was really upset, and I did not want that to interfere with the conversation I needed to have with these young men." After sitting down with the young men, Fleming learned that the dispute was the result of a girl who had a reputation for breaking up friends. "I helped them realize that they both had gotten played," Fleming said. "Even though they apologized to one another, I was very disappointed because they were my leaders. They had a cohort of underclassmen who looked up to them." These young men are no different than anyone else who finds themselves in difficult situations. Sometimes no matter how much someone knows, emotions can interfere with rational thinking.

Early in my career, I coached a young man named Jamal. Jamal was a great athlete and a born leader. He was naturally gifted and talented in so many things. As a result of his natural abilities, he appeared to exert minimal effort on the field and in the classroom. His ability to do so well without trying creates a rude arrogance at times. This behavior was exhibited during his interactions with his teammates and coaches, which were frequently inappropriate. His negative engagement with his teammates was something that caused me a great deal of distress. I knew how tremendous of an influence he had with his team. This influence was not respected and often caused the team to suffer when his behavior was unfavorable. After watching Jamal almost self-destruct and create unnecessary chaos in his life, I felt compelled to do something. As a mentor, I had to intervene before things got really bad for him.

Changing the trajectory of Jamal's life became a mission for me. I wanted desperately to find a way for Jamal to see his potential, on and off the field. I invested countless hours, resources, and energy in helping him transform into the leader I knew he could be. I tried everything I knew how to do but it was producing minimal results. Even worse, Jamal became such a menace to the coaches and his teammates that he was eventually cut from the football team. Not too long after Jamal was expelled from school and forced to enroll at an alternative school. An alternative school is typically an environment for youth who exhibited great learning and behavioral issues. Jamal did not belong there. Nothing I tried to do for him succeeded and ultimately, Jamal declined in his behavior. His choices and inability to engage in his success cost him a great deal. As a mentor, I was crushed and still feel horrible about it.

Although Jamal's situation became less than favorable, that experience did teach me a few things. The first thing I learned is that mentors cannot force success on their mentees and we cannot save everyone. It showed me that no matter how much we want our mentee to do well or make better choices in life, they must share the same desire. They have to be willing to invest just as much time and commitment into their lives as we do. Which brings me to another lesson that I learned from this situation. Mentors should never give more to the process than their mentee is willing to give. The level of interest and dedication must be the same.

Understanding these concepts are important for mentors to learn. As adults, we have limited resources and time is one of our most precious resources. We have families, careers and a life outside those we mentor. So mentoring anyone should be accessed like a financial investment. We have to try and decipher early if the return on the commitment is going to be worth it. We must invest in mentees who present less risk of disappointment and who promise a gratifying return. That means initially we must secure their individual buy-in to the mentoring process. We should ask ourselves these questions. Are our goals in sync? Are they willing to do the work needed to succeed? The more honest we are in the beginning, the less pain we will feel in the end. Minimizing disappointments in the mentoring process is so essential that I developed four principles to gain success in that area. These principles have helped me tremendously once I figured them out. They will surely bring you great success as well.

1. Start broad, finish narrow.

When my schedule allows time for a mentee, I start broadly to determine if there is a young person who is seriously interested in my areas of expertise. Those areas are leadership and entrepreneurship. I express these areas of strength when I volunteer at schools in various capacities or when I participate in speaking engagements. Through either of those interactions is when I typically attract young men who want to know and understand more. They begin to express their interest in becoming a leader and or entrepreneur.

Those that express an interest in learning usually bombard me with questions more than others. They show me that they are really listening to what I am saying and want to know more about it. Just being a listener is not enough for them. They want to be engaged in the conversation. When I notice young men inquiring more, I transition them to a smaller group to gain more clarity on what they want to know. I help them take a deeper dive into their thoughts and try to be as honest as possible. I prefer this approach because, in small group settings, I am able to learn more about the students. When it is less of them, I focus on discerning who they are individually and how to help them. This makes it much easier to start developing their skills to achieve success.

2. Reward according to merit.

My second principle evolved from a mentoring relationship with a highly intelligent young man named Jose. Jose is very funny and charismatic. He is also a very gifted artist. Between José's artistic talent, his personality, and his motivation to find a job, I saw great potential for success in him immediately. I could see his determination and knew that if I worked with him, my time and effort would not be wasted. So I connected with him instantly. I became a fan of his. I was so impressed with the things José had going on. His gifts almost distracted me from his personal life. Jose was so dedicated and eager to learn because he was going to be a young father in a few months. This revelation triggered a sense of urgency to help him even more. We began diligently to help him find gainful employment.

In an effort to help Jose as much as possible, I dived right into finding out what he needed to be better. Jose's main priority right now was to find employment so he could support his family. This was the only goal he wanted to work on with me. In the initial meeting with Jose, I found out that he had some challenges that made it difficult to achieve this goal. Jose did not finish high school and he did not have a GED certificate. This was a huge but not impossible obstacle to overcome. I found a job fair that was happening soon that I wanted him to attend. He agreed and appeared eager to get started. We both had the understanding that the minimum requirements to attend this event was to be enrolled in a general education degree program. Noticing that the requirement was to be enrolled and not already have the certificate gave some hope that this could work.

I began diligently searching for open programs for him to start and I found one. It was a program starting at a local community college. Understanding how urgent this need was for him, I personally drove him to the school for registration. He was ready to start building the next phase of his life and was now qualified to attend the fair. I arranged for transportation for him to the job fair because he stated this was an issue for him. Someone was scheduled to pick him up early that morning, take him to the fair and drop him back off at home once done. We seemed to have solved every problem that was in his way from achieving his original goal. Everything was looking encouraging. Until the day of the fair, Jose did not show up. His ride was there on time and ready, but he never came out of the house. There was no communication from him on that day at all. He also never attended the GED class we registered for as well. I was crushed.

I was furious with myself and with him. I could not understand what happened. He gave me a goal he wanted to achieve. I provided all the support to achieve that goal. And then he did not follow through. I tormented myself for not recognizing the lack of commitment on Jose's part in achieving his goal. I could not understand that he knew completing his GED was essential to him finding employment to provide for his family, yet he did not follow through on it. How could someone so talented and charismatic not care? Jose expressed his dreams and aspirations to me that tugged on my heart. His desires sparked something in me that was compelled to help him get there. I did not comprehend why he just did not show up. I did so much to put him in the right position. I had to realize that my work was the problem. I invested more in his journey than he did. So I stopped. I never followed up with Jose after that.

A few weeks later, Jose contacted me. He was still in need of my help. I was invested in continuing to see him win, so I did, but my approach was different. Now I had the understanding that now my role as a mentor was not to do his work for him but to provide him the resources he needed to achieve his goal. This time I explained that he had to dedicate his time and effort into the process. And if he wanted me to invest my time or effort to help him, he was going to have to prove that he was willing to help himself first. My time was a gift that I wanted to provide as a reward for him making personal gains. Once he made a step on his own, only then would I reward his effort with my time.

In response to his renewed request for job search help, I gave him flyers and contact information to conduct his search on his own. I did not spend time facilitating his searches for him, nor did I organize his transportations to get there. I put the success of Jose in his hands. I was there to guide and provide resources to support him. Our relationship was different. Although he understood and appeared interested, Jose still did not put in the work. This was a difficult experience for me because I wanted so much for him. In empowering him to do more for himself, he chose not to. After some time had passed, I randomly saw Jose at a grocery store; he informed me that he was working at a car wash. While I was glad he had a job, I knew he is capable of so much more.

3. Mentors are influencers, not dictators.

Let me stop for a moment to address the issue of parenting and mentoring. In many cases, parents are partners in mentoring relationships. But it has been my experience when mentoring Black and Latinx male teens; parents are sometimes peripherally involved or completely disinterested. Being engaged in the lives of your mentees can be difficult. You should know and understand every aspect of their lives. You should know and connect with their parents/guardians.

I typically know very little about my mentees' home lives. In some cases, it is because they do not want me to meet their parents. Perhaps they are embarrassed or do not have a healthy relationship with their parents. Either way, it causes a missing component in the healthy development of the youth. That void could foster dependency or fantasy that I am the dad they never had. Although caring and investing enough into a young person's life that they consider you worthy enough to be a parent, it is actually not a healthy scenario. Boundaries can be crossed, lines could be blurred and expectations can come unrealistic. It is up to the mentor to set those parameters in place to ensure that the relationship dynamics are understood at all times.

Working with young men in small groups helps me accomplish that. I recommend that approach for maximum effectiveness and minimum complications. This is important especially if you have not established a relationship with the parents or even have been introduced to them. Teens do not need to have parental permission to be engaged in a group with peers. So it is not uncommon to work with a young person and never meet their parents. Please take precautions in spending so much time with a young person—particularly one-on-one—without a parent knowing who you are and what you are doing. This can land a mentor in big legal trouble.

"Mentors are not parents and we do not dictate what they should do," Vondale Singleton reminds me. "At most, our task is to give them direction. Our mentees may or may not choose to follow our suggested path. Our role is not to be an enforcer. However, when they do stray from the path, we should be there to motivate, teach, and encourage them to stay the course and achieve their goals."

Having an excellent partner relationship with at least one of the mentee's parents provides dual support for the young man. Home can also reinforce the guidance you are providing if you all are partnered in the process. This extra layer of support is beneficial for everyone. Parents stay with your mentee more than you are and they can monitor progress more frequently. Having a good relationship with a parent should be a goal but it still does not mean that the mentoring relationship will succeed. It helps to cultivate a greater chance for them to achieve their goals, but the choice to put in the work necessary for success is up to the youth. Sometimes nothing you do, no one you partner with or no matter how many great opportunities you provide, things just do not work out. It is a hard reality but it happens. This is why I developed the fourth principle: *Know when to leave the relationship.*

4. Know when to leave the relationship.

After struggling on occasion to pull a young man over the finish line, Ray McElroy has helped me come to a realization that not everyone can be helped. He developed the understanding that even he may not be able to save every single boy. Accepting that reality, he says, took humility. "I can expose them to all the best stuff on the planet; I can share all the principles. I can have the best speeches and videos. But ultimately, it's their choice to open their hearts, receive the information and jump all the way in, or reject it. If Jesus didn't convert everybody, I guess I need to have some perspective that I may not. But, I can go to sleep at night knowing that I gave it everything I had."

CHANGE THE RULE

We desperately want our mentees to succeed, as I did with a young man I will call George. He had all the skills, resources, and parental support to be successful. For extra measure, I also built a strong relationship with his mom, who welcomed the presence of a strong male mentor in George's life. However, his friends and poor decision making were holding him back. This caused some challenges in his progress. George was in college. He had planned to attend summer school and had secured a job on campus. Then one day, he just uprooted himself and moved to a neighboring state to pursue a job opportunity there. This decision was a surprise to his mom and I. We had no idea where this shift came from. He did not land the job, which left George with moving and living expenses he could not pay. He was now far away from home with no help. His sudden and irrational decision cost him unnecessary stress.

I often feel that George expected the adults in his life to fix his messes. I believed he considered this to happen, especially with his mother, who was extremely supportive of him. Often when I meet with him, he would make an emotional plea for help. He would always tell me about a mistake he made and how he wanted to change. In every plea, there was always a request for money. At first, I gave him small amounts because I believed in him. Then I realized that nothing was improving. No matter how much I tried and gave, it was not good enough. In fact, things were getting worse. For example, George landed on academic probation, which resulted in a loss of financial aid. So he needed someone to cosign a loan so he could stay in school.

Despite his requests, his mother and I both agreed that we were not going to do that. We both refused to incur any financial liability for someone who exhibited irresponsible behavior and decision making. In fact, George's inappropriate request was the straw that prompted me to end our relationship. It was not healthy for us to continue because no one was benefiting from it anymore. I began to feel like my efforts were not appreciated. My role was being seen as a provider instead of a mentor. I could no longer help this young man. Although it is never easy to end any relationship, it is even harder to hold on to one that causes pain. I share this story because when you give a mentee too much, too early—whether it is your time, your connections or even cash—without having to work for it, you cripple their work ethic and you build an unrealistic expectation that you will do what they are not willing to. Some younger generations seem to have an unrealistic expectation of life or a sense of entitlement.

This perspective can be extremely difficult to endure. The mentoring process with someone that feels they are entitled to something can become cumbersome. This is something that a mentor must reprogram about their mentee's expectations. The best thing a mentor can do for any young person, especially for one with this mentality, is to teach them that nothing in life is free. You always have to work for what is worth having.

Discussion Questions

1. What is the difference between an Influencer & a Dictator?

2. What are some ways we can positively influence our mentee's?

3. Why is it important to connect with your mentee's parents or guardian?

4. Is it acceptable to end a Mentorship relationship? Why or why not?

5. What are some effective ways to encourage your mentee after they made a poor choice?

WALTER MENDENHALL IV

CHAPTER 5

How to Create Boundaries

Mentors and mentees should negotiate boundaries carefully because, while having no boundaries can harm the relationship, having too many can incapacitate it.

~ L. J. Zachary

I launched into mentoring with great enthusiasm, not realizing that those who lead with the heart should proceed with eyes wide open, and with a full understanding of our motivations. In my case, I wanted to be everything to my mentees—the attentive father they never had or the big brother they may have wanted. These are not bad qualities to have, but we just have to understand what motivates us to mentor fully. When we understand why, then we can guard our hearts more when dealing with relationships.

In my case, I learned that I wanted to be everything to my mentees. What motivated me was to become the person that left a void in their life. I wanted to be their attentive father they never had or the big brother they may have always wanted. I just wanted to provide emotional support, stability and direction in any way I could to the young men I served. Although I meant well, in retrospect, I realize that this was not healthy. I was an earnest young man trying to fill all of the gaping holes created by my own father's neglect during my youth. I sincerely did not and still do not want other young people to carry the pain I felt at that age. So my mission became trying to avoid them from experiencing this type of pain I endured during childhood.

After some time of mentoring many young men, I now know that this was a misguided mission. I tried to be everything to everyone, and I failed miserably. Good leaders are unrelenting learners. We learn some of the most important lessons from our mistakes. I definitely learned a lot from mine. As leaders, it is important for us to know ourselves and motivations before we embark on the mentorship path. This helps us understand our true motivations on wanting to be a mentor. Sometimes our underlying reasons for mentoring are hidden in our subconscious minds. Being unaware of this can increase the likelihood that we will misguide not only ourselves but also others. Consequently, we would do everyone a favor if we took some time to do some self-reflecting and inner healing before we begin to help others.

Self-reflection is healthy for everyone but especially for those leading others. This is because someone else's life is in our hands. We cannot approach this lightly. If once we reflect and discover that we may be leveraging mentorship as a bandage for our wounds, it is probably best to step back. We cannot effectively heal a young person if we are not healed ourselves. Our mentees have different needs and desires. When becoming a mentor, the mentees' needs should come before ours. When we are not healed, this can not occur. I have learned to be focused, secure and certain when committing to a young person. I want to be able to meet their needs and be capable of setting healthy boundaries that support a successful mentoring relationship. These guidelines helped me to have healthy boundaries with my mentors. They have been great for me and I know they will help you as well.

1. Ration your time.

Mentoring requires a sacrifice of time. For many, it requires time that could be devoted to their own families. How do you reconcile that? Singleton suggests enlisting all family members' support. "I explained to my kids, 'Hey, Daddy has a major call on his life to help young African American and Latino boys. I cannot do it without your support. This is how you can do that for me. I need to be able to leave from 9:00 am until 1:30 pm every Saturday. If you give me that time, I promise nothing will go undone here at home. I will not neglect you. I will still do my duty." My wife chimed in, "Yeah, you still have to take the trash out and handle the laundry." After establishing boundaries at home, he then sets boundaries with his mentees. "I let the young men know the window of time that I have set aside for them. I let them know my wife and kids need me too. That is really, really important."

This concept became very important to me as well so I also set specific boundaries. I learned to protect my personal space and home life over time. I do not answer calls or text messages after 9 p.m. Being always available resulted in my mentees calling and sending text messages late nights and early mornings. This was fine with me until I got married. Not only did I have to allocate my time more efficiently, but I also wanted to give my bride the respect, peace and attention she deserves. These days, I may not respond to a text for a day or two, unless it is an emergency. Otherwise, I am very specific about my hours to be contacted.

Sometimes emergencies do arise and I handle them all accordingly. When young people are concerned, they feel that everything is an emergency when it is not. They just want your attention when they want it. Then there are times when they really need your help. For example, one of my mentees called me at 3:00 am one winter. He had worked the late shift at UPS and was unaware that the bus did not operate 24 hours. He ended up walking seven miles to his home from work and was stopped by the police. The officers were holding him at the station. Since no one in his family had a vehicle, I was his only hope. In this situation, I did not hesitate to come to his aid. Without hesitation, I went to pick him up from the station. By contrast, when another mentee traveled out of state and contacted me for money for a hotel room in the middle of the night, I did not respond. I know my boundaries and I stick to them.

2. Never be alone with a mentee.

We all have read the headlines and watched the documentaries regarding inappropriate contact between youth and adults. Teachers have been caught engaging in inappropriate contact or sexual abuse in various situations all over the country. When adults and minors meet outside the classroom or programs, it leaves the door open for boundaries to be crossed. Whether interactions were intentional or not, strengthened guidelines have been developed to protect both parties. This is why mentors have to be more conscious about their level of engagement with mentees. For that reason, I strongly suggest against being alone with a mentee as much as possible. Although sometimes it can be unavoidable, we should try our best to adhere to it.

On those rare occasions, I have had to establish some standards to operate in to keep everyone safe. In order for me to be alone with any youth, they must fall under this criteria. My mentee must be over the age of sixteen, I must have a relationship with his parents, and I would have been mentoring him for at least one year. Otherwise, outings with mentees usually involve at least two young people at all times. If you unfortunately find yourself alone with your mentee or any young person, always keep the door open. This will allow anyone to have clear access to your space and be witness to no inappropriate behavior occurring. I know some may want the door closed for privacy concerns. This is definitely understandable. You just have to weigh your options and hopefully choose to be better safe than sorry.

3. Limit physical contact.

When interacting with young people, especially those of the opposite sex, it is up to you to establish physical boundaries. Even innocent physical contact can unknowingly trigger a bad memory for some people. Many young people have been sexually or physically abused. Even an innocuous touch on the arm can be a reminder of a painful experience. This is why I limit initial contacts with young people to a handshake. After I get to know them and they know me, we may greet each other with a short casual hug. Even then, I typically allow the youth to initiate it. I never want to invite myself into any form of uncomfortableness for them.

Sometimes my speaking engagements or group sessions may include girls. It is not preferred for me but depending on the environment, I may have to welcome it. When this happens, I am extremely careful about my interactions with them. When they become comfortable with me, they too want to embrace sometimes. When this occurs, I only allow them to give a side hug. I remember a time when I co-led a coed mentoring group with a woman facilitator. There was a male student that shook my hand or gave me a short embrace. When he encountered the woman facilitator, he wanted an extended hug from her. She noticed it as well and began developing a strict boundary with all students from there. She decided to no longer allow hugs in the group.

Teens are like children in some aspects. They both want to know how far they can push a boundary. They want to test you to see if you are consistent or if you are willing to stand your ground. This happened to me once during a field trip downtown on a hot summer day. A group of teens and I had been walking outside for an extended period of time. A young lady asked if I could carry her on my back. My response was a definitive, "Absolutely not!" My quick reaction and stern tone made her understand that she had crossed a boundary. I had to be tough on her at that very moment because I had to reinforce boundaries that were set in the beginning. I had to remind her and everyone else that there is a clear line between their interactions with me and their peers. They had to see me differently and respect my boundaries. They are in place to respect and protect everyone.

4. Use positive language.

Being careful with our physical boundaries is very important when working with youth. It is also important to be careful of our verbal language. Respect can be gained and lost, depending on how we communicate. Healthy communication is more than just actual verbiage but also the delivery of messages. I never use profanity or yell at my mentees. I model this behavior because I do not want them to behave like that with me either. Young people are bombarded daily with negative, disrespectful, and dehumanizing words. I do not want to become one of those people. My goal is to always create safe and nurturing environments for them. They thrive in these types of spaces. I would never take that emotional, social and mental space away from them.

Negative communication, obscene language and derogatory phrases were things you would hear kids in the past. It was not something that adults participated in freely and was frowned upon. Today it is exhibited almost daily on social media; they almost cannot escape it. This behavior has become normal for most of us. I want them to know that meanness and incivility are not normal or acceptable. I do not allow young people in my presence to speak negatively to or about each other. By the same token, I perform the same behaviors with my teens. I always address them as mature young adults, not as children. Words such as "stupid," "dumb," "goofy," or "ignorant" do not cross my lips. I set a high standard of behavior and hold an expectation that we will all treat each other with mutual respect. It's not always easy, especially when I am refereeing in basketball games. Competitive sports can bring out the worst in people.

There have been times when young men have called me names or cussed at me. Some even wanted to fight me and anyone else in their way. There also have been times when I have raised my voice to invoke my authority, reminding them that they are speaking to an adult. On those occasions, I ordered the disrespectful students to leave and invite them to return when they can behave more maturely. I also have ended games abruptly because the young men were not adhering to the rules and standards of conduct I have set.

Being consistent with this expectation and continuously using positive language has helped me gain respect from the teens. I became known for being the adult in their lives that will not disrespect or demean them. When there are times their behavior was less than favorable, it did not take them long to apologize. When I have to remove a teen from my program for negative behavior, it typically does not last longer than a week for them to return. They always apologize and I always accept. I always accept apologies because I want to model forgiveness over retaliation. I also hope they will mirror that understanding when conflicts arise elsewhere. I use every opportunity I can to teach my teens life lessons that they can use everywhere and everyday.

5. Don't be an ATM.

As a novice mentor, I was determined to make a positive difference in young people's lives, no matter what. If they needed the shirt off my back or money from my pocket, I wanted them to know I was there for them. It was no hesitation for me to provide whatever they needed. I even helped a mentee purchase a car before which has to be the highest-ranking mistake I have ever made in mentoring. At the time, I thought I was helping by lowering a hurdle he had that was holding him back. What a huge mistake.

His name was Marquis. He needed a thousand dollar down payment to purchase his car and I gave it to him with some conditions. I only required him to keep his job, continue his education, and pay me a minimal amount of money for the loan. He already was employed at Walmart and was enrolling in prerequisite courses at a two-year college so he could apply to a university. With those boxes checked, I figured he would adhere to them and maintain his part of the deal. I figured that nothing would go wrong. Within a few months, Marquis left (or was asked to leave) his job. He never attended classes at the city college nor took the entrance exam for the university. To make matters worse, he eventually totaled his car in an accident.

Needless to say, Marquis could not reimburse the money he borrowed from me. He then left town to live with his mom. Although I was extremely disappointed, Marquis taught me an important yet expensive lesson. That lesson was to never give money to a mentee. Sometimes mentees really experience hard times and are in need of financial assistance. Now, instead of providing them actual cash, I will happily purchase something for them that is a necessity. I will buy food, clothes and other important items. I will sponsor school trips or pay a school-related fee directly to the school. I will even buy a bus pass. I will never place actual cash in another mentees hand. Period.

I desperately urge you to learn from my mistake instead of making yours. As mentors, we cannot fix every situation or every broken child. When we give a mentee more than basic necessities, which are wise counsel, an empathetic ear and humanitarian aid, we can foster an unhealthy mentoring relationship. We could potentially create an expectation that there are easy fixes to situations that cause teens to learn how to endure through tough times. We do not want to stifle their growth from always applying bandages to cases that need surgery.

Discussion Questions

1. Why are boundaries important in a mentoring relationship?

2. Why is it important to assess your motives for mentoring?

3. What specific boundaries do you need to create to have a proper life balance?

4. How can you establish realistic expectations with your mentee?

CHAPTER 6

UNLOCKING THE SHACKLES

"They have limited exposure to and understanding of their possibilities, and do not believe in themselves or see beyond today."

~ Derrick Fleming, Jr. College Access for Chicago Scholars.

Exposing young men to new ways of thinking is as important as exposing them to new environments. Or, as the motto of the venerable mentoring juggernaut, 100 Black Men of America, phrases it: "What they see is what they will be." Perceiving an urgent need for black boys in New York's most financially weakened communities to see that people who look like them can succeed in America is monumental to future aspirations for youth. In 1963, Jackie Robins and a group of black professionals and industry leaders set out to do just that. They wanted to improve conditions in New York's low-income areas by changing the trajectory of the young men who resided in these communities. They wanted to provide role models and programs to help these young men envision and create better outcomes.

Since that time, "The 100" original members have evolved into more than 100 chapters throughout the country. Their 10,000 plus members have impacted more than 125,000 lives. That is outstanding, to say the least. Since then, many share the mission to make a positive difference for youth of color. Among them is Rickie Clark, who has designed, implemented and engaged with numerous youth programs for the past thirty years. Some of his program affiliations were youth entrepreneurship programs and My Brother's Keeper, which is an initiative of former President Barack Obama. "In order to be a man, you must see a man," Clark told me during our interview. One of his organizations engages college fraternities with high schools, matching teens with men of color. It is an outstanding program that helps adults hold youth accountable for their success.

In My Brother's Keeper, there are levels to engagement and impact. The college graduates help the high school seniors persevere through various situations. The current undergraduates help middle school students with their needs. High school seniors even interact with elementary school students through reading programs. "My goal is to offer them a variety of tools to remove the barriers of isolation and limited thinking. I want to inspire young people to have a grander vision for their lives," Clark stated. That is such a transformative mission. If kids in an impoverished neighborhood only see people generating income by selling drugs, that becomes a "normal" income opportunity. Exposure to different skills provides new choices. It provides them with a better outlook on life.

Many may argue that youth cannot use their environment as an excuse to not be exposed to something different because of the availability of choices through the internet. Although the knowledge of more is available, it does not compare to what they see when they are looking out the window. What is virtual may not register as anything real or possible for them to achieve, compared to the reality they face daily. This is why they need mentors who can offer personal guidance and help them navigate the world against a headwind. They need to meet men who look like them and are successful in life. They need exposure to business owners, managers and executives in major corporations; men who travel to faraway places and lead lives in contrast to those they encounter in their neighborhoods. They need to see positive possibilities in life.

This experience could inspire them to break free of the shackles of poverty by completing high school, pursuing a certification in a lucrative trade, join the military or even obtain a college degree. Even if a prospective mentor does not have direct knowledge about empowering networks such as the 100 Black Men of America, they have access to something that could be used to motivate the youth to achieve more. There are other organizations, churches and community groups that can provide the needed resources and support. There is always something that can be done for them and people who are capable of getting it done.

I try to provide my youth with everything they need by connecting them to any opportunity I see as valuable to their growth. When I learned that a church on the West Side of Chicago was planning an annual tour of historically black colleges and universities (HBCUs), I asked for fifteen of my young men to be included. A similar tour broadened my horizons when I was young. During my senior year in high school, our football coach took my younger brother and I to a half dozen Midwestern colleges. It was tremendously inspirational. Not only did we finish college, but we both also made it to the NFL. My brother, Rashard, had a long career in professional football and I completed a master's degree.

That experience ultimately changed my life. So when I heard of something similar that would do the same for my youth, I did not let that opportunity slip away.

The church welcomed my mentees to participate in the event but I would have to pay for their admission. The cost for fifteen of them to attend the five-day experience was $7,500. That was a lot but I was not going to let that be a barrier. I felt it was important for them to attend this trip so that they could see colleges that were established after slavery for and by people who looked like them. If any of these young men chose to attend college, they would be the first in their family to do so. Plus, they would receive incomparable support through a HBCU. HBCU faculties and administrators understand where the students are coming from, they relate to what these students are going through and they care about their success. So I was determined to raise the required funds by asking people within my network. And I did just that.

In true mentor spirit, I did not just give them a golden ticket to this all-expense paid experience. I wanted them to put in some work in order to show me they were invested in this event. I required students who wanted to attend to write an essay explaining why. One student's essay really touched my heart. He wrote that he had never been on a college campus or out of the state of Illinois. While that applied to most of my students, this young man lived in a public housing development. He wanted to set an example for his family members and neighbors by attending college. That very tenacity is exactly what I wanted to see from them. So I, of course, selected him to attend with fourteen other students.

This experience was a week-long road trip across several states. We visited four historically black universities— Southern, Dillard, Xavier and Jackson State, and two colleges—Rust and Lemoyne. Our group really bonded after spending so much time together. The teens learned more about each other than they had during the years they had spent in school together. We discussed race relations, systematic oppression and the meaning of manhood. They even asked questions to get to know me on a deeper level. They asked me specific questions about why I became a mentor and why I use my resources to help young people. It provided a platform for my mentees to hear me in a way they never had before.

On this trip, I expressed my heart and explained my motivation for doing this work with them. I explained that when I looked at them, I saw myself at that age. I saw a young man whose father was mostly absent and consistently financially, physically and emotionally unsupportive. A man who had a mother that worked long hours to keep food on the table and a roof over his head. I saw young people who needed love, encouragement and support. The only reason I am where I am today is because people took an interest in my life. Teachers and coaches saw my worth and encouraged me to aspire to achieve great things. I grew up thinking that's what teachers and coaches do, so it was only natural for me to do the same.

I am compelled to make the same kind of investment in young people's lives that was made in mine. I challenged my mentees often to do the same for others when they achieve life goals. Give back to those behind you. They need you more than you know. I hope I honor my mentors every time I help a young person. I certainly feel honored and proud whenever a mentee takes a step in the right direction because of something I said or did. It moves me to continue to do more and be present when there is minimal support for a young person. It solidifies my life's work.

Everyone that went on the HBCU tour applied for admission to one of the schools we visited or indicated that they planned to apply. While that outcome exceeded my expectation, it did not always work out that way in other situations. As I learned after taking another student on a college tour previously. His name was Damon. I had coached Damon on our school's football team since his sophomore year. Unlike most young men living in his tough neighborhood on the west side of Chicago, Damon had a big long term goal. He wanted to play football at Stanford. This goal motivated him to stay out of trouble, which required considerable effort in his environment. It also inspired him to work hard in the classroom and on the field. Damon was not the most talented player on the team but he was one of the toughest and most determined. By his junior year, he had a 3.8 GPA. This was a huge accomplishment for a young man who had repeated eighth grade after moving to Chicago from Alabama. It was commendable indeed.

Damon's father was disabled. His mother supported the family on her minimum wage income. Despite these adversities, his parents attended every game and came to know my wife and I quite well. So when I asked my wife if Damon and I could tag along with her on an upcoming business trip to northern California, she instantly agreed. His parents were grateful and deeply moved by our generosity. They, too, wanted Damon to realize his dreams were possible. We traveled to Palo Alto, California. It was an eye-opening experience for him. This experience naturally led to conversations about culture and environment. More specifically, a lot regarding appropriate attire and disposition. This unexpectedly stirred up some difficult conversations about life.

Damon strolled through campus with a hood over his head until I made him understand that some people are uncomfortable around black males wearing hoodies. I explained that his attire could determine a lot of how people perceive him. He is a black man in a predominantly white world traveling on a predominantly white campus. Although this was new for him, I quickly let him know from experience that he must always be conscious of others perceptions. In today's society, it can literally be the difference between life and death. I shared a principle I had learned in college called "double consciousness." Double consciousness is when, as a man of color, we must be aware of how we view ourselves. We must constantly gauge how other nationalities view us. Often, these perceptions do not coincide. It is an unfortunate but realistic situation for African Americans across the United States.

During our time there, I could tell that Damon was having difficulty adjusting to that environment. Plus, our trip made him aware that even though he may have been academically prepared for college, he was not at the level of scholar-athletes that Stanford recruits. Damon was not discouraged by this. He pushed forward and landed a full academic and football scholarship to a college in Wisconsin. Although it was not the fulfillment of his initial dream, his success inspired me to continue exposing male teens of color to a variety of opportunities. They deserve to be aware of all educational, professional and non-traditional experiences. Everyone is different and thrives in a different environment. Whatever needs to be done to help a young person achieve their dreams, we as mentors must help them maneuver the obstacles to success.

I am a firm believer in helping youth get out of their comfort zone and exposing them to more. It does not have to be just college exposure. I have taken my teens sailing, visited professional business settings such as Google's Chicago headquarters, investment firms, hospitals, and numerous post-secondary opportunities. I also introduce them to the power and possibilities of entrepreneurship. Most young men lack the tools or knowledge for building a business. This is why I founded the Male Mogul Initiative program, which offers leadership and entrepreneurship development to teens in under-served communities. My hope is that no matter what we expose them to, it will expand their thinking on what is possible. It is my hope that it will inspire or motivate them to become catalysts for positive transformation in their lives and communities.

There have been some young men in my program that stood out amongst the rest. Among them is a young man I mentored for three years. His name is Maurice. It has been exciting to watch Maurice blossom. He has combined the entrepreneurial skills he learned in MMI with his natural leadership ability and created a profitable business. Maurice and his MMI cohort's first venture was a T-shirt business. It was not just any T-shirt business. They wanted to take a product to market that could change the perception of young black men on Chicago's West Side. They branded their T-shirt line "Young Heroes." Under Maurice's leadership, the cohort developed a business plan to become a highly visible positive force in their community.

They engaged in a number of community service projects. They picked up garbage on the streets and even read to kids in local schools. Whenever they were doing good in the neighborhood, they wore all their "Young Heroes" branded merchandise. They also sold their shirts online. To demonstrate their commitment to the mogul mindset, the group entered the Network for Teaching Entrepreneurship's (NFTE) business pitch competition at Northwestern University, and Of course, they won! After completing the MMI curriculum, Maurice's cohort dissolved their "Young Heroes" business. He later transferred the presentation and sales skills he had learned into launching his own T-shirt company.

Since his launch, Maurice has generated thousands of dollars of revenue. This is proof that when we take an interest in the lives of young men of color, it makes a difference to them. Making a difference to them individually overall contributes to a change in the society. How many generations of young men never fulfill their potential? How many become prisoners rather than productive citizens because they could not effectively handle their emotions, had low self-worth, were insufficiently educated and had no hope for a happy future? The number is countless. This is why it is so important to invest time in another person. It can prevent not only a life of disappointment for them but others impacted by their lives as well.

As an African-American male from a single-parent home with limited resources, who was labeled with a learning disability, I know the helplessness our young men feel. I conquered it with help. Most do not. The invaluable support and encouragement from my mentors fueled my dedication to education. They transformed me into the motivated, accomplished and determined man I am today. Growing up, my mom would tell me, "You are destined for greatness. The only person that can stop you is you." And I say the same to you and any young person that we encounter.

I encourage you to invest the time and energy needed to change the course of someone's life. This generation needs people who can give them wisdom, make a positive impact in their lives, love and affirm them like a parent. They need someone to believe in them and show them the way to be better. They need more than just a role model on the television, that is physically untouchable. They need you. They need a mentor who will be there to walk through life hurdles with them daily. If you are reading this book, and you feel that this is what you were called to do. Your heart is in it. You have a passion for uplifting others. You believe you can guide another person to success in all areas of their life. I commend you for embarking on this journey and I know those you're positively influencing will too. I trust that you are destined for mentoring greatness. The only one who can stop you is you. So enjoy the ride and take plenty of notes on your journey!

Discussion Questions

1. "What they see is what they will be." What does this quote mean to you in the context of mentoring?
2. In your words, what is the responsibility of a mentor?
3. What are the major takeaways you got from this book?
4. What is your plan for guiding your mentee to success?

www.ingramcontent.com/pod-product-compliance
Lightning Source LLC
Chambersburg PA
CBHW021412290426
44108CB00010B/491